SHEENAH HANKIN, PH.D., was named one of New York's most popular psychotherapists by the *New York Times Magazine*. The codeveloper of Cognitive Appraisal Therapy, she received her graduate training in counseling from Aston University in Birmingham, England. She is the coauthor of *Succeeding with Difficult Clients* and has been featured as an expert on personality and confidence on national television and in publications such as the *New York Times*; *Newsweek*; *Vogue*; *Redbook*; *Elle*; *Allure*; *O, The Oprah Magazine*; and the *New York Post*. Dr. Hankin has conducted workshops all over North America and Europe. She lives in New York City.

COMPLETE
CONFIDENCE

Also by Sheenah Hankin, Ph.D.

Succeeding with Difficult Clients
(with Dr. Richard Wessler and Dr. Jonathan Stern)

COMPLETE CONFIDENCE

A HANDBOOK

SHEENAH HANKIN, Ph.D.

HARPER

NEW YORK • LONDON • TORONTO • SYDNEY

HARPER

A hardcover edition of this book was published in 2004 by ReganBooks, an imprint of HarperCollins Publishers.

FIRST PAPERBACK EDITION PUBLISHED 2005.
FIRST HARPER PAPERBACK PUBLISHED 2008.

Designed by Kris Tobiassen

Hand illustration by Adam Walko

The Library of Congress has cataloged the hardcover edition as follows:

Hankin, Sheenah.
    Complete confidence : playing the game of life with a winning hand / Sheenah Hankin.
       p. cm.
    Includes index.
    ISBN 0-06-009647-0 (alk. paper)
    1. Self-confidence. 2. Self-actualization (Psychology) I. Title.

BF575.S39H39 2004
158.1—dc22   2004041785

ISBN 978-0-06-154454-5 (updated edition)

08 09 10 11 12 WBC/RRD 10 9 8 7 6 5 4 3 2 1

In loving memory of my brother,
Peter John MacKenzie, 1947–1996

CONTENTS

COMPLETE CONFIDENCE